Fast and Slow

Also by John Ciardi
I MET A MAN

Fast
and
Slow

Poems for Advanced Children and
Beginning Parents

By JOHN CIARDI

Illustrated by Becky Gaver

Houghton Mifflin Company Boston

Several of the poems in this collection have appeared
previously in magazine form. They are: WHY THE SKY IS BLUE
and ON SOME DAYS I MIGHT TAKE LESS in *Cricket;*
SUZIE'S NEW DOG in *The Saturday Review;* and FAST AND SLOW
in *The Saturday Evening Post.*

Library of Congress Cataloging in Publication Data

Ciardi, John, 1916-
    Fast and slow.

    SUMMARY: Thirty-four humorous and nonsense poems,
including "A Fog Full of Apes," "A Fine Fat Fireman," and
"I Should Never Have Trusted That Bird."
    [1. Humorous poetry. 2. Nonsense verses]
I. Gaver, Becky, ill.   II. Title.
PZ8.3.C52Fas   811'.5'2   74-22405
ISBN: 0-395-20282-5 REINFORCED EDITION   ISBN: 0-395-26680-7 PAPERBACK EDITION

PRINTED IN THE UNITED STATES OF AMERICA

V   10 9 8 7 6 5 4 3

To Mrs. G. B. Erskine,
our beloved Connie

Table of Contents:

Fast and Slow

Fast and Slow

The old crow is getting slow.
  The young crow is not.
Of what the young crow does not know
  The old crow knows a lot.

At knowing things the old crow
  Is still the young crow's master.
What does the slow old crow not know?
  — How to go faster.

The young crow flies above, below,
  And rings around the slow old crow.
What does the fast young crow not know?
  — Where to go.

And on Some Days I Might Take Less

There was a man who lived in Perth.
He had about five dollars worth
Of boys and girls at three-for-a-dollar.
The less they were worth, the more they would holler.
The more they would holler, the less they were worth.

For two cents' cash I'd send you to Perth.

CAT--
BEWARE!

~SNICK!

Suzie's New Dog

Your dog? What dog? You mean it? — that!
  I was about to leave a note
Pinned to a fish to warn my cat
  To watch for a mouse in an overcoat!

So that's a dog! Is it any breed
  That anyone ever knew — or guessed?
Oh, a Flea Terrier! Yes indeed.
  Well now, I *am* impressed!

I guess no robber will try your house
  Or even cut through your yard.
Not when he knows you have a mouse
  — I mean a dog — like that on guard!

You have to go? I'm glad you came!
  I don't see a thing like that
Just every day. Does it have a name?
  Fang, eh? Well, I must warn my cat.

A Fine Fat Fireman

A fine fat fireman ran up the ladder.
  He blew out the fire with a fine fat puff.
He reached for the lady. He almost had 'er
  When the ladder decided enough was enough.

Snap went the first rung. *Snap* went the second.
  Down came the fireman, fine and fat.
He landed on the chief. The chief hadn't reckoned
  On anything as fine and as fat as that.

Down flew the lady. She lost a slipper
  And three gold pins when she landed in the net.
Down slid the fireman like the handle of a zipper.
  The chief lost his ladder. (He hasn't fixed it yet.)

Down went the chief with his helmet dented.
  He woke with the fireman sitting on his head.
He spoke to the fireman. They haven't yet invented
  All of the words for what he said.

Some of his words had sparks at the center.
     They floated up the wall — floated higher and higher.
They reached the lady's window. The lady saw them enter.
     Half a minute later they restarted the fire!

Up jumped the fireman, fine and fat.
     He climbed the wall. He puffed out the blaze.
The lady kissed the fireman. "A man like that
     Is the man for me for the rest of my days!"

The chief fired the fireman. The fireman quit.
     "Huff and puff for yourself," said he.
"This work's too hot by more than a bit."
     And he married the lady and he went to sea.

Now he's a sailor, a fine fat salt.
     The lady has new gold pins. (Slippers, too.)
If your helmet's dented it's your own foolish fault.
     Don't stand under ladders. You'll be sorry if you do.

On Being Too Right to Be Polite

When I was a boy I was so good
   People for miles around
Would crowd into our neighborhood
   And wait without a sound

From dawn to dark and half the night
   And then again next day
For a chance to watch me be polite
   And, perhaps, to hear me say:

"Please" and "Thank you" and "Howdjado?"
   And "Would you be so kind?"
And "Oh, how very good of you!"
   And "Really, I don't mind."

And to watch me serve the ladies tea
   And help them with their coats.
Some people filled up two or three
   Large notebooks full of notes

On being good. One wrote a book
   On what he learned from me.
So many came that at last I took
   To charging a modest fee.

From dawn to dark and half the night
   And then again next day,
A nickel to watch me be polite.
   A dime to hear me say

"Please" and "Thank you" and "Howdjado?"
   And "Would you be so kind?"
And "Oh, how very good of you!"
   And "Really, I don't mind."

In a year or two and a day or two
   I became a millionaire.
And the best of that (as, of course, you knew)
   Is that no one seems to care

About your manners when you're rich.
   And the rich care even less.
And that's my tale, the moral of which
   I should think even you might guess.

The Shark

My dear, let me tell you about the shark.
Though his eyes are bright, his thought is dark.
He's quiet — that speaks well of him.
So does the fact that he can swim.
But though he swims without a sound,
Wherever he swims he looks around
With those two bright eyes and that one dark thought.
He has only one but he thinks it a lot.
And the thought he thinks but can never complete
Is his long dark thought of something to eat.
Most anything does. And I have to add
That when he eats his manners are bad.
He's a gulper, a ripper, a snatcher, a grabber.
Yes, his manners are drab. But his thought is drabber.
That one dark thought he can never complete
Of something — anything — somehow to eat.

Be careful where you swim, my sweet.

And They Lived Happily Ever After for a While

It was down by the Dirty River
    As the Smog was beginning to thin
Because we had been so busy
    Breathing the worst of it in,

That the worst remained inside us
    And whatever we breathed back
Was only — sort of — grayish,
    Or at least not entirely black.

It was down by the Dirty River
    That flows to the Sticky Sea
I gave my heart to my Bonnie,
    And she gave hers to me.

I coughed: "I love you, Bonnie.
    And do you love me true?"
The tears of joy flowed from my eyes
    When she sneezed back: "Yes — Achoo!"

It was high in the Garbage Mountains,
    In Saint Snivens by the Scent,
I married my darling Bonnie
    And we built our Oxygen Tent.

And here till the tanks are empty
    We sit and watch TV
And dream of the Dirty River
    On its way to the Sticky Sea.

Here till the needles quiver
    Shut on the zero mark
We sit hand in hand while the TV screen
    Shines like a moon in the dark.

I cough: "I love you, Bonnie.
    And do you love me true?"
And tears of joy flow from our eyes
    When she sneezes: "Yes — Achoo!"

Questions! Questions! Questions!

What do you know? It's going to snow.
How can you tell? By sniff and by smell.
What do you sniff? The wind off the cliff.
What do you smell? The ice in the well.
What do they say? It's coming this way.
How deep will it be? Two fathoms or three.
What shall I do? Stay here till it's through.
What shall I eat? Ox tail and pig's feet.
Where shall I sleep? In the pen with the sheep.
What if it gets colder? Put a lamb on your shoulder.
What if it melts? You can go somewhere else.
Then what will I get? Your feet good and wet.
How will I dry them? Bring them here and I'll fry them.
What of my dad? He'll say they taste bad.
What of my mother? She'll cuddle your brother.
What about you? I'll be glad when you're through.

I Am Writing This at Sea

I met your father yesterday. He asked me what I thought
About the price of lettuce seed. (It has gone up a lot.)
He asked if I liked baked beans cold. (I certainly do not.)
He told me he had some for sale and if I liked them hot
He would be more than happy to sell me a bean pot.

I told him I had two at home and one aboard my yacht.
That brought us round to sailing, a subject that soon
brought
The talk around to fishing and the big ones we had caught.
And after we had lied a bit (as fishermen will do)
We found we had no more to say, and so we talked of you.

I told him you were very good when you were good at all.
He shook his head and sighed and said he couldn't quite
recall
The last time you were any good except that week last fall
When you were home in bed with grippe. I said I'd heard
you bawl
When you had to take your medicine. He said, in general,
He'd rather row an elephant to Salem in a squall
Than put up with your antics when you start to caterwaul.
But we agreed you eat quite well, and that when you were
small
You weren't as wide as you are now, nor — certainly —
as tall.
That left us with no more to say, and so, as usual,
I bought my beans, put them aboard, and sailed off with
the tide.
And he cast off my lines for me, and then went home and
cried.

On Learning to Adjust to Things

Baxter Bickerbone of Burlington
Used to be sheriff till he lost his gun.
Used to be a teacher till he lost his school.
Used to be an iceman till he lost his cool.
Used to be a husband till he lost his wife.
Used to be alive — till he lost his life.
When he got to heaven Baxter said,
"The climate's very healthy once you're used to being
    dead."

Bear with Me and You May Learn

The strangest bear I ever saw
Was back in eastern Arkansas.
   He was polka-dotted yellow and blue
   On day-glow pink with a purple shoe
On — I think — his left hind paw.

This bear I saw — that I *think* I saw —
Had three green whiskers on his jaw.
   His ears were red. His tail was white.
   As bears go, he was quite a sight,
Even in eastern Arksansas.

He swam the river to Tennessee,
Leaving a trail I couldn't see.
   It's hard to trail a swimming bear.
   When you look for his tracks, they're just not there.
Yet, where else could they be?

He swam the river and turned it green
With orange stripes, and in between
   Those stripes were some in yellow and blue,
   And one the color of chocolate goo
That was very hard to clean.

The sheriff came from Arkansas.
He caught the bear by the left hind paw —
    A rather shrewd thing for the sheriff to do.
    That, you recall, was the paw with the shoe.
So the bear just couldn't claw.

The sheriff came from Arkansas.
He caught the bear by the left hind paw.
    He put him in jail and he left him there.
    I'm not at all sure he was being fair,
But a bear like that is against the law.

He stayed in jail for a year and a day.
When they let him out, he ran away
    And hid in the woods. The woods turned red
    And yellow and brown. "Oh! Oh!" he said,
"I've done it again!" And he had, I'd say.

The sheriff came to trail the bear
For changing the woods. There was no trail there.
    Or if there was, the leaves came down
    And colored it red, and yellow, and brown.
And the bear was gone — I don't know where.

The sheriff hunted according to law
Through every county in Arkansas.
    He hunted here. He hunted there.

He never found a trace of the bear.
Not so much as the print of a paw.

The sheriff said: "I must catch that bear
Or he'll color the whole world wrong. Now where
   Could he have gone? According to law
   A bear that isn't in Arkansas
Must be somewhere else. I must look for him there."

So the sheriff hunted, according to law,
Through all the states *around* Arkansas.
   He saw six states before he was done.
   You already know Tennessee is one.
Can you name five more the sheriff saw?

He looked for seven days and a night.
— At least he did when the sun was bright.
   He saw all the states around Arkansas.
   Once you have named the states he saw,
Can you draw them for me and color them right?

P. S. He never caught the bear.
I'm glad he didn't. I don't care
   If the bear *did* get his colors wrong.
   He tried his best as he went along.
And that's good enough. What's fair is fair!

On Going to Hohokus (and Why I Live in New Jersey)

From Peapack to Hohokus
    Is really not too far
Unless you start from somewhere else.
    It depends on where you are.

I went from Lower Squankum once
    Through Bacon's Neck and Hopatcong
With a stop at Cheesequake, but I think
    That way's a bit too long.

It's longer from Piscataway
    Across to Tuckahoe
With a detour through Buckshutum.
    Still, the main thing is to go.

And if you really don't know why
    But somehow feel you should,
Wear tight shoes: when you take them off,
    Your feet will feel so good

You can't help being happy there,
    Though when you think about
Having to start back, you may wish
    You hadn't started out.

I'll Let You Know If I Find Her

Molly O'Golly lived in Mount Holly
   In a house on a street with a cat,
And a roof on the house, and a puppy (a collie)
   Named Jolly O'Golly. And so much for that.

For the cat ran away and Jolly O'Golly
   Stopped being a puppy. (That happens, you know.)
His fifteen grand-puppies still live in Mount Holly
   But Molly got married and down came the snow.

It covered the roof of the house in Mount Holly.
   It covered the steps and the street. It came down
And covered the tracks made by Molly O'Golly
   When she and her husband left town.

In the spring when it thaws I may go to Mount Holly
   To look for the footprints they left in the snow.
I'll trail them, by golly, until I find Molly.
   I'll write you about her. — That is, if I go.

A Long Hard Day

There was a man from Delaware
    He took a pig to market.
He drove a jeep. When he got there
    He found he couldn't park it.

He let the pig get out and wait
    While he found a place to park.
The nearest was in New York State.
    When he got there it was dark.

He sent the pig a telegram:
   "Where are you? Please reply."
The pig wired back: "I think I am
   About to leave. Goodbye."

The pig went back to Delaware
   And married a fine young sow.
I hear they are still living there
   And have twelve piglets now.

The man was tired. He went to sleep.
   When he got out of bed
He dressed and tried to start the jeep.
   The battery was dead.

He kicked its tires and left it there.
   It may be parked there still.
He never came back to Delaware.
   I doubt he ever will.

Some Sound Advice from Singapore

There was a man from Singapore
Who dressed in everything he wore
And took a walk along the shore.

The shore was right beside the sea.
Mostly — or so it seems to me —
Because of nowhere else to be.

For the same reason as before
The sea was right beside the shore.
As for the man from Singapore.

His reason was: If you take care
To dress in everything you wear,
You won't get sunburned walking bare.

The Man Who Had Shoes

When I went down to Newport News
    For a stroll around the Square,
I met a man who had no shoes.
    At least, his feet were bare.

"I have one for the left and one for the right
    And an extra pair of laces."
He said to me, "But they're so tight
    I never wear them places.

"For shoes cost money and feet are free."
    — There's something to think about.
"Why wear them into town," said he,
    "Only to wear them out?

"Sometimes when I am home at night
    I put them on and try
A step to the left, a step to the right.
    But then I sit and cry.

"For when I think how dear they were
    And about how tight they are.
It comes to me that I prefer
    Bare feet for going far.

"When I leave home I leave them there
    Under the bed with my wife,
As good as new. With proper care
    They will last me all my life.

"And that is why I walk in skin
    When I want to stroll about.
For if I only wear them in.
    I cannot wear them out."

Why Noah Praised the Whale

The elephants on Noah's Ark
    Ate seven bales of hay
For forty days and forty nights
    — Seven whole bales a day!

Two hundred eighty times in all
    As he pitched another bale
The animals heard Noah cry,
    Thank Heaven for the whale!

"I like my elephants, of course,
    But once our trip is done,
They will be fat on Ararat
    And I'll be skin and bone

"From pitching hay day after day,
    Bale after dusty bale.
And that is why I often cry,
    Thank Heaven for the whale!

"It's bigger than the elephant
    But wise creation gave it
A safe snug sea, and that saves me
    The bother of having to save it.

"It saves itself. With elephants
   I have to do the saving.
And that's a thought I think a lot
   When I am down here slaving

"To pitch them hay day after day,
   Bale after dusty bale.
And that is why I often cry
   Thank heaven for the whale!"

Well, Welcome, Now That You're Here

The little hand was straight across.
   The big hand was straight down.
That's how I knew what time it was
   When you first came to town.

The sun was on the attic floor
   Just touching the bamboo cane
I hung on the knob of the closet door,
   When you first came again.

I heard you ring. I heard you knock.
   I heard my hash-hound bark.
I took him out for a very long walk.
   When we got back, it was dark.

The moon came up in the dogwood
   And into the windowpane
(The third from the right) and it shone so bright
   I heard you come again.

The moon came up through the dogwood
   As bright as a TV screen
On a night in June when it won't quite tune
   But only shines to be seen.

33

The moon climbed up through the dogwood
   Dragging a star or two,
When I heard the bell, and I said "Well, well!"
   For I knew it had to be you.

So I let you in, as you knew I would,
   And I knew you had come to stay.
— Which isn't too bad. No, it isn't too good,
   But welcome anyway.

You can sleep in the hall — it's a good soft floor —
   And keep your eye on the clock.
When the big hand touches a quarter to four
   And the little one ticks the tock

Of half past six, the moon will be down.
   The sun will start to climb.
When it reaches the wall across the hall
   You must telephone for the time.

And wake me up at ten past eight.
   And since you are here to stay,
I'll have eggs with ham and toast with jam.
   You may bring it up on a tray.

And when I have eaten and had my shower
   And written another rhyme,
I'll waste a quarter of half an hour
   In trying to teach you the time.

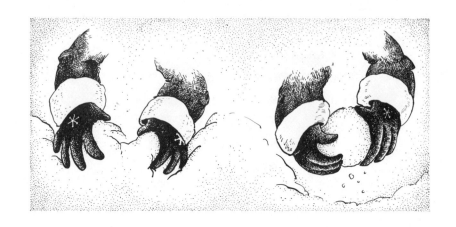

Read This with Gestures

It isn't proper, I guess you know,
   To dip your hands — like this — in the snow,
And make a snowball, and look for a hat,
   And try to knock it off — like that!

We All Have Thought a Lot About You

Two hundred twenty thousand, five hundred
    twenty-three
Registered local voters (well, yes, including me)
Were asked to vote in secret on what to do with you.
Two hundred twenty thousand five hundred twenty-two
Voted to put you in a cage and throw away the key.

That isn't quite unanimous, but I think you will agree
That as a test of sentiment their vote will surely do
To indicate what seems to be a rather general view
Shared by the mayor, the aldermen, your teachers, the
    police,
The deputy dog-catcher, the man who makes the keys,
The man who makes the cages, and the keeper of the zoo.
You might say everyone in town — no, that's not strictly
    true —
But *almost* everyone in town takes a dim view of you.

Why the Sky Is Blue

I don't suppose you happen to know
Why the sky is blue? It's because the snow
Takes out the white. That leaves it clean
For the trees and grass to take out the green.
Then pears and bananas start to mellow,
And bit by bit they take out the yellow.
The sunsets, of course, take out the red
And pour it into the ocean bed
Or behind the mountains in the west.
You take all that out and the rest
Couldn't be anything else but blue.

— Look for yourself. You can see it's true.

He Lived, Alas, in a House Too Big

There was a man who lived in a house
   A big White House with a fence around it.
He lost his way from room to room.
   And nobody ever found it.

He picked up the phone and called the police.
   "Please come to my house and find me."
"Where are you?" they said. "I'm in one of my rooms
   With the rest in front and behind me.

"I'm in one of my rooms on one of my floors
    With the rest in front or behind me,
Except for those above and below.
    If fifty men can't find me

"Send fifty more. I'll phone the cook
    To feed them pork and beans.
If you haven't found me by New Year's Day,
    I'll phone for the Horse Marines."

That was in January, I think,
    About three years ago.
A hundred police and the Horse Marines
    Ate up ten tons or so

Of pork and beans, then ten tons more.
    And twenty of pancake pie.
The horses ate forty tons of oats.
    The cook began to cry.

The man kept phoning from room to room.
　　The cook kept phoning the store,
Said the man on the phone, "Have you found me yet?"
　　Said the cook, "Send ten tons more."

Said the hundred police and the Horse Marines
　　Whenever they answered the phone,
"Can you look around and see where you are?"
　　Said the man, "I am here, and alone."

They finished the pork. They finished the beans.
    They finished the cook — she quit.
Now the phone keeps ringing in her room
    But nobody answers it.

A hundred police and the Horse Marines
    Are running around and around
Looking for something else to eat.
    And there's nothing to be found.

Not pork and beans. Not pancake pie.
    Not a cup of dishwater tea.
Not even the man they came to find.
    Whoever he may be.

If he ever turns up from wherever he is
    In the big White House with the fence around it.
He is in there yet, but he lost his way
    And nobody ever found it.

When Happy Little Children Play

When happy little children run
   To skip and dance and play,
I often stop to watch their fun,
   And to smile when I hear them say:

"You skunk! You louse! You rat! You brat!
   Shut up! Get lost! Yah-yah! Drop dead!
Says who? Oh, yeah? If you say that
   Once more I'll split your head!

How sweet their voices and how dear
   The way they skip and dance!
It makes me wish their dads were here
   To warm the seats of their pants!

The Family Reunion

I spoke to a gorilla who asked me about you.
I said I didn't know you. (Well, I'm not glad that I do.)
He said he was your cousin. I could see that it was true.
A very distant cousin, he explained. I couldn't see
That he looked very distant — not from *your* family.
He asked the way to your house. At first I wouldn't say.
I begged him for his own sake to continue on his way.
(Why mislead a poor gorilla into having to go through
The things I have to suffer when I come to visit you?)
He insisted. I evaded. He grew angry. I grew scared,
For I noticed he was snarling hard and that his fangs
    were bared.
So I told him how to get there. What else could I have
    done?
Have you been home at all today? If not, you'd better run.
Your cousin said he couldn't stay. He is just passing
    through
On his way to take a new job at the San Diego zoo.
And he mentioned most especially he would like a look
    at you.
I said that was no problem — his own looking glass
    would do
For a general description. He supposed that would be
    true.

He said family resemblances should come as no surprise,
But that he'd like to see you, if just once, with his own
    eyes.

Well don't just stand there gawking with your bare face
    hanging out!
Your parents must be calling you. I think I hear them
    shout.
Your cousin's waiting for you to get home. You'd better
    run.
It's a family reunion and you mustn't miss the fun.

What Johnny Told Me

I went to play with Billy. He
Threw my cap into a tree.
I threw his glasses in the ditch.
He dipped my shirt in a bucket of pitch.
I hid his shoes in the garbage can.
And then we heard the ice cream man.
So I bought him a cone. He bought me one.
A true good friend is a lot of fun!

Thanks Anyhow

When I was a boy in your town
   I lived on wax and cheese.
I got the cheese from a billy goat.
   I got the wax from bees.

Dinner with a billy goat.
   Breakfast with the bees.
What's for lunch? — Banana peel.
   But first you must say please.

Dinner was bad and breakfast worse.
  Lunch was, alas, a mess.
I tried the food at your house.
  I liked it even less!

Dinner with a bunch of brats.
  Breakfast at the zoo.
Never mind lunch — I'd rather munch
  Cardboard than eat with you.

49

Captain Spud and His First Mate, Spade

Tough Captain Spud and his First Mate, Spade,
    Were saltier than most.
They followed the sea (that being their trade)
    From coast to coast to coast.

From coast to coast to coast is about
    As far as a sea can reach.
Once you sail in, you have to sail out,
    Or you'll be on the beach.

Not Spud and Spade. They made their trade
    Wherever they happened to be.
And just as soon as the trade was made
    They put back out to sea.

And once they were safely under way
    They'd start a squabble or two
To pass the hours of the lonely day,
    As good friends often do.

They sailed with a cargo of Yo-yo strings
    Hand-woven in the Highlands,
And traded for bottle caps and things
    In the far-off Sandbox Islands.

They sailed to where the Gum Trees grow
  And traded the caps for prizes:
Tin whistles, jacks, and balls of wax,
  And ten-for-a-penny surprises.

Said Spud to Spade as they loaded the hold,
  "Some swindler in this crew
Has swiped my genuine plastic-gold
  Space Badge — and I mean you!"

Said Spade to Spud, "You're much too quick
  With your fingers. That ball of twine,
And seven feet of the licorice stick
  You have in your pocket are mine!"

Said Spud, "I have eyes in the back of my head,
  And I'm watching you, old mate-oh!"
"That's how it is, old Spud," Spade said,
  When your head is a potato.

"It has eyes in front that cannot see.
  And eyes in back that are blind.
And nothing inside, as it seems to me,
  That might pass for half a mind."

And so, as good friends often do.
  They bickered night and day,

And treated themselves to a squabble or two
  To pass the lonely day.

So they grew rich in the Yo-yo trade,
  And testier than most.
— As you'll hear men say of Spud and Spade
  In the jungle gyms of the Coast.

For Spud was a salt, and Spade was a tar.
  And both were sea-going men.
Till they took to going to sea so far
  They never were heard of again.

Riddle

What do you do when you're up in a tree
And start to climb higher, when what do you see
But a Snaggletooth Scratch with a wart on its nose,
And a growl in its throat, and claws on its toes
Just waiting up there and looking at you,
Well, maybe, for nothing better to do,
And just licking its chops to pass the time?
Well, maybe. But anyway, back you climb.
And as soon as you're sitting safe on a branch
You happen to see a Hooknose Granch
Taking the view from the end of a limb.
And the view it is taking is, mostly dim.
And, mostly, of you. And full of hooks,

And clacking beaks, and hungry looks.
So you start to climb higher. And what do you see
But the snout of a Snarling Shivaree
With its forked tongue out, all drooly and twitchy,
And its nose wrinkled up as if it were itchy,
And a claw reaching down? — and you understand
It isn't trying to hold your hand
And invite you to pass the time of day,
And hope you feel you would like to stay
To be lunch, or dinner, or just a snack?
— Well, you can't climb up, and you can't climb back.
So now for the riddle: what do you do?

Give up? Yes. I think I would, too.

I Should Never Have Trusted That Bird

When I was last at Seaside Heights,
    Out walking on the bluff.
The wind was flying sixty kites.
    Said I, "There's wind enough

"For sixty kites and sixty more."
    I sent a crow with sixty cents
To buy them for me at the store.
    It flew off past my neighbor's fence.

I waited sixty days or more.
    The wind began to fail.
"If I ever see that crow," I swore,
    "I'll put salt on its tail.

"I'll tie a string around its toe
    And fly *it* for a kite.
My sixty cents is lost, I know,
    But *that* will serve it right!"

Fast Isn't Far

There was a boy with a souped-up car.
He drove it fast but not too far.
Just up to a curve he didn't quite make,
And through the fence, and into the lake.

Pets

I once had a wolf and a bobcat
    I kept for the friendly way
They would claw and yowl and snap and growl
    — Like you when you come to play.

I bought them a boa constrictor
    To cuddle them tenderly.
When it squeezed too tight they would claw and bite
    And put the blame on me.

The cat was squeezed to kitten size.
    The wolf was squeezed to a pup.
Then the boa unpinned its jaws and grinned
    And winked as it swallowed them up.

It swallowed them up. It swallowed them down.
    Then it napped for a week or two.
Then it climbed a tree, and it looked to me
    As if it were looking for you.

If it does show up at your house,
    I hope you make sure it gets fed.
If I am right, you will know tonight
    When you look under the bed.

If it isn't there, you must wait till it comes.
    If it is, I hope you won't cry.
If it starts to squeeze, will you phone me, please?
    I'd hate not to say goodbye.

A Fog Full of Apes

Ninety-nine apes with their tails on fire
   — Well, two were just starting to smoke —
Came yammering down from a tree to inquire
   If someone was playing a joke.

I don't really know why they came to ask *me*
   — I had happened to just happen by
When apes started pouring down out of the tree
   Demanding to know what and why.

"Gentlemen! Gentlemen! Please, this won't do!"
   I cried. "Things are all in a muddle!
I suggest you sit down, and the best seats for you
   Might be there — in that rather large puddle."

They sat in the puddle. It started to steam.
   The steam spread and covered the sun.
In the dark I could hear them yell, holler, and scream:
   "Who did this?" and "What has been done?"

I hope I won't seem too deceitful and sly
   If I tell you I ran off and hid.
You'll recall I had happened to just happen by
   When whatever was happening did.

I had, I submit, done as much as I could.
    I had acted the part of a friend.
And heated debate would have done much less good
    Than the puddle had done — in the end.

Yes, they would, I was certain, cool off — in the end.
    But what if their tempers stayed hot?
An ape, I am told, is an uncertain friend
    When he happens to think you are not.

It really won't do to go blundering through
    A fog full of apes to protest.
You're bound to find one who starts snarling at you
    And beating his fists on his chest.

I left various lotions (and bandage and tape)
    By the puddle. And then, well — I ran.
It is well to do good, and best to escape
    From the good you have done — while you can.

I Hate to Wait

Someone came to see me when I was not at home.
I let him in and told him I was sorry he had come
On just exactly almost the day I wasn't there.
So we made an appointment to meet again somewhere.
I think we said last Tuesday noon at quarter after eight.
He said he'd be there on the dot but that he might be late.
I said if he was there on time I would be glad to wait.
I even told my mother I was going to meet him there.
But now it's Thursday morning and I can't remember
    where
I was supposed to meet him. I know he hasn't come.
I'll give him ten more minutes. And then I'm going home.

64

Flowers

A flower that no one ever saw
May not have bloomed at all, and yet
In Zanzibar or Arkansas
Or Tanganyika or Tibet
Or anywhere you care to be
There are more flowers than you can see.

An unseen flower is hard to know.
What color is it? And what size?
How far would someone have to go
To find it — if he had good eyes
And looked all day? And when he found it,
What of the other flowers around it?

I doubt that all the flowers there are
Could have been found by anyone.
Some of them blossom much too far
From anything (except the sun)
For all the finders there could be
To go out looking for, and see.

A lot of flowers (of course) bloom where
A lot of people happen by.
But even when you see them there,
And even if you really try,
Do you suppose, from Spring to Fall,
That anyone could see them all?

Of course not, not if everyone
Went everywhere there is to go
With flowers blooming by the ton.
When they were gone, a flower would grow
Behind them and remain unseen.
And that flower is the one I mean.

It's pink, it's blue, it's red, it's white.
It lasts a day or two or three.
It nods and dances in the light.
And, yes, the chances are, a bee
Stops by and drinks a taste of sweet.
The sun goes by and sends it heat.

The day goes by, or two, or three.
And before anyone could know it,
Whatever flower there used to be
Goes out as seed. The breezes blow it
From here to there to start again
Next year, or next. But even then

No one could hope to see them all.
The red, the white, the pink, the blue.
Not sun-flower big, nor grass-bud small.
And yet *all* flowers must be true.
If there are more than we can see,
That's not too many flowers for me.